Who Was
Ernest Shackleton?

Who Was
Ernest Shackleton?

by James Buckley Jr.
illustrated by Max Hergenrother

Grosset & Dunlap
An Imprint of Penguin Random House

GROSSET & DUNLAP
Penguin Young Readers Group
An Imprint of Penguin Random House LLC

Text copyright © 2013 by James Buckley Jr. Illustrations copyright © 2013 by Max Hergenrother. Cover illustration copyright © 2013 by Penguin Random House LLC. All rights reserved. Published by Grosset & Dunlap, an imprint of Penguin Random House LLC, 345 Hudson Street, New York, New York 10014. The WHO HQ™ colophon and GROSSET & DUNLAP are trademarks of Penguin Random House LLC. Printed in the USA.

Library of Congress Control Number: 2013032703

ISBN 978-0-448-47931-6   10 9 8 7 6

This book is dedicated to young
explorers eagerly heading out
on their own adventures!—JB

This book is dedicated to my my wife and son.
Thank you for giving me the time to create my art.
You are the most loving and supporting family
I could ever ask for.—MH

Contents

Who Was
Ernest Shackleton?

In 1914, Ernest Shackleton was the leader of
a voyage to the South Pole. It was the third time
he had made such a trip, but he had not reached

the Pole itself yet. He had returned safely from the other journeys. This time, however, he didn't know if he would make it back home to England.

Shackleton sat stranded at the bottom of the world. He and his abandoned ship, the *Endurance*, were trapped. He watched helplessly from camp as the ship was slowly crushed by ice. He and his crew were more than a thousand miles from human contact. Shackleton had no way to call anyone for a rescue. The men were running out of food and the temperature would only go down.

Once the ship was crushed and then sank, Shackleton and his crew were alone in the icy wasteland of the Antarctic. Over the next six months, they would defy the odds time and again. Under Shackleton's leadership, the men battled cold, hunger, ice, wind, and loneliness. They had to find food in a barren land. They made two amazing trips in open boats. They worked together to survive, day after day.

In they end, they won. Shackleton, one of history's most amazing leaders, brought all twenty-seven members of his crew safely back home.

Shackleton's courage and his crew's incredible journey made him one of the most famous Antarctic explorers ever. How did they ever make it back from such a desolate, cold, and lonely place? And why did they want to go there in the first place?

Curiosity, adventure, and bravery all played a part in the life of a man whose crew called him simply "The Boss."

Chapter 1
Off to the Sea!

Ernest Shackleton stood on the bow of his mighty ship. The wide green ocean spread out in front of him. The wind whistled through his hair. "That way, men!" he called to his crew. "There's adventure ahead!" He couldn't wait to see what was out there.

Suddenly, a voice came from the ocean.

"Ernest! We have to go!"

The young boy was not really on the ocean, but on the huge lawn in front of his house in Ireland. His "ship" was a giant log in the grass. The voice came from one of his sisters, and it really was time to go. Ernest and his family were leaving for another adventure in a new home.

Ernest Shackleton was born in Kilkea, Ireland, on February 15, 1874. He lived in a large house on an Irish farm until he was six. On his wooden "ship" or in the nearby woods, Shackleton and his pals spent hours as pirates or ship captains or explorers.

Ernest had a large family. He had a brother named Frank, and he also had eight sisters! Being a farmer with ten kids was very difficult for Shackleton's father, Henry. So when Ernest was

six, Henry moved the family to the city of Dublin, Ireland.

While his father returned to school to become a doctor, Ernest studied at home. He and his siblings were home-schooled by a governess, who is a live-in teacher.

Ernest found time for adventure, however. Once, he dug a huge hole in their small back garden. He declared that he was going to dig to Australia, on the other side of the world. He got some of his ideas from the *Boy's Own Paper*, a magazine for young readers filled with stories of explorers, soldiers, and exotic foreign lands.

After Henry became a doctor, the family moved to London, England. And for the first time in his life, at age eleven, Ernest had to go to school.

At Fir Lodge, his first school, he was often teased. He and his family were English, though he had been born in Ireland. Because of his Irish accent, the other students called him "Micky," an insulting nickname for an Irish person. But Ernest just laughed. In fact, friends and family later called him Micky, too.

At his next school, Dulwich, he played sports

such as cricket and boxing. In later years, his
friends remembered that he always stuck up for
kids who were being teased. He and his friends
read sea stories together because that's what
Ernest found most exciting. Ernest realized that
a regular school was not for him. Later in his life,

he wrote, "I wanted to be free. I wanted to escape from a routine which didn't at all agree with my nature. . . . Some boys take to school like ducks to water . . . but for a few rough spirits, the system is chafing, not good, and the sooner they are pitched into the world, the better. I was one of those."

Soon the call of the sea was too strong. In 1890, at the age of sixteen, with his parents' help, Ernest got a job as an apprentice seaman.

For the restless Ernest Shackleton, it was time to leave boyhood behind. Adventure awaited at sea.

Chapter 2
A Hard Life, but a Good One

Shackleton shipped out on the *Hoghton Tower*, a merchant vessel. He was sixteen, but he was treated like a grown man. He hauled ropes, carried heavy loads, and worked in all kinds of weather. Shackleton worked so hard lifting bales of rice and hauling ropes that his hands ached. He had a hard time even holding a pen to write letters home. He also had to climb the huge masts high above the sea. As the ship rocked back and forth and the wind blew, Shackleton clung to the ropes and did his job.

It was a hard life, but Shackleton found the adventure he was looking for. He sailed to Chile. And he eventually visited India and the island of Mauritius. After one of his trips, he returned home. His sisters decorated their London home with welcoming flags. Shackleton presented them with baby alligators that he named Faith, Hope, and Charity. (When

the babies grew too big for the backyard pond, they were donated to the London Zoo.)

By the time he was twenty-two, he had reached the rank of first mate, a rank second only to a ship's captain. He learned how to steer ships and about cargo, sails, and engines. As his ship took

short hops around Europe, he learned how to live in a small space with many men, most of whom worked for him. Men who sailed with Shackleton in those early days remember how good he was at being a leader.

But trips to nearby ports were not enough adventure for him. Part of the reason Shackleton wanted more was his love of exploring.

The other reason was simply love.

In 1897, during a visit home, he had met Emily Dorman. They both loved poetry and

came from big families. During his visits, they went to museums together. Over time, they fell deeply in love. Shackleton knew that he wanted to marry Emily, but he felt that he had to be more successful and have more money. If he went on an important ocean journey, on his return he might earn money writing and speaking about his adventures. He could be paid for being a hero.

Then, in 1900, Shackleton read a newspaper article that changed his life.

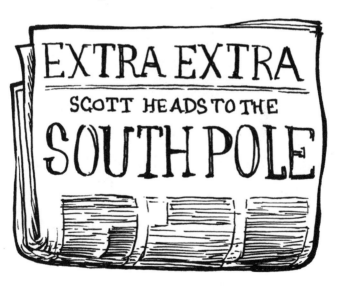

EXTRA EXTRA

SCOTT HEADS TO THE

SOUTH POLE

Chapter 3
Sailing with Scott

In the summer of 1900, English naval officer Robert Falcon Scott was chosen to lead a journey to the South Pole, a place no one had ever reached. After reading about Scott's plans, Shackleton very much wanted to go on that trip. Through a friend, Shackleton got a job on Scott's crew.

Before he left, he wrote to Emily's father. He asked his permission to marry Emily when he returned. Ernest Shackleton left on his first big trip to the South Pole with a happy heart.

On Scott's ship, *Discovery*, Third Lieutenant Shackleton was in charge of supplies and the crew's entertainment. He even packed wigs and dresses for the crew to use to put on plays! Shackleton shipped a typewriter, too. He used it to write the *South Polar Times*, a shipboard newspaper.

RACE TO THE POLE

NORTH POLE

SOUTH POLE

IN THE EARLY 1900S, THE TWO POLAR
REGIONS WERE AMONG THE LAST SPOTS ON
EARTH THAT REMAINED UNEXPLORED. FOR
CENTURIES, MEN IN SHIPS HAD SAILED THE
WORLD, CLAIMING DIFFERENT LANDS FOR THEIR
HOME COUNTRIES. THEY WANTED TREASURE,
WOMEN, TRADE, AND GLORY. BUT THE TWO
POLES REMAINED UNTOUCHED. NEW SHIPS THAT
COULD BREAK THROUGH THE ICE AROUND THE

POLES HELPED OPEN THE WAY TO THEM. MANY MYSTERIES REMAINED, HOWEVER. HOW COLD WAS IT? WAS THERE LIFE ON THE ICE? WERE THERE MOUNTAINS, CANYONS, AND HILLS?

UNLIKE EARLIER EXPLORERS, POLAR ADVENTURERS WERE NOT SEEKING TREASURE OR CONTROL OF THE LAND. THEY SIMPLY WANTED THE HONOR AND FAME OF GETTING TO THE POLES FIRST.

IN 1909, TWO AMERICANS, ROBERT PEARY AND FREDERICK COOK, EACH CLAIMED TO HAVE BEEN THE FIRST TO REACH THE NORTH POLE. ENGLAND LED THE WAY IN TRYING TO BE FIRST TO REACH THE SOUTH POLE. AS DIFFERENT TEAMS MADE THEIR ATTEMPTS, PEOPLE BACK HOME FOLLOWED THEIR ADVENTURES CLOSELY. MILLIONS OF PEOPLE WONDERED WHO WOULD BE FIRST.

The *Discovery* reached Antarctica in January 1902. The ice surrounding the continent soon surrounded their ship, too. They were trapped until it thawed out. Scott told his men to set up camp on the thick ice.

Shackleton helped plan the camp. He made sure the men had food and clothing. After they were settled, he helped with scientific experiments. Always ready to try something new, he became the first man to take aerial photos of Antarctica from a hot-air balloon.

In November 1902, Captain Scott prepared to make the long walk from their camp to the South Pole. He chose two men to join him: Ted

HOW DID THEY FIND THE SOUTH POLE?

EXPLORERS LOOKING FOR A PARTICULAR ISLAND KNOW EXACTLY WHEN THEY COME UPON IT. ADVENTURERS WHO "DISCOVER" A MOUNTAIN KNOW EXACTLY WHEN THEY ARE STANDING IN FRONT OF IT. BUT FOR TRAVELERS TO THE POLES, IT IS MUCH MORE DIFFICULT TO KNOW FOR SURE THAT THEY'VE REACHED THEIR DESTINATION. THERE ARE NO LAND FEATURES OR SIGNS. IT IS A SURFACE WITHOUT LANDMARKS, WHERE ALL YOU SEE IS "WHITE." TO KNOW IF YOU'VE REACHED A POLE, YOU NEED TO BE AN EXPERT AT NAVIGATION AND THE USE OF SCIENTIFIC INSTRUMENTS.

SEXTANT

COMPASS

THE NORTH AND SOUTH POLES ARE THE END POINTS OF AN IMAGINARY LINE THAT PASSES THROUGH THE CENTER OF THE EARTH. TO FIND THOSE END POINTS, EARLY EXPLORERS MEASURED THE DISTANCE OF THE SUN FROM THE HORIZON USING A SEXTANT TO LOCATE EXACTLY NINETY DEGREES SOUTH LATITUDE. THEY ALSO RELIED HEAVILY ON COMPASSES TO SHOW DIRECTION. WITHOUT THE ABILITY TO MEASURE TRAVEL SPEED OR DETERMINE A STRAIGHT LINE, THERE WOULD NEVER HAVE BEEN AN ACCURATE WAY TO PINPOINT THE POLES.

Wilson and Shackleton. The trio packed food and gear and set off for the unknown heart of Antarctica—the very bottom of the world.

The men walked for about two months. They pulled sleds and made camps on the ice amid wind and blowing snow. It was extremely difficult. They had not brought enough food. Shackleton fell sick, and Wilson thought his companion was dying. They trudged on, however, hoping to reach the Pole.

Finally, Scott made the hard decision to head back, even though they had not reached the South Pole. After they arrived safely back at the camp, Scott insisted that Shackleton go home on a relief ship. Shackleton didn't want to go and later complained about how Scott had treated him. For years afterward, the two men were rivals. Scott thought that Shackleton had not been strong enough for the trip. Shackleton thought that Scott was not a good enough leader. Even with all they

had survived together, the two men did not part as friends.

On his first big adventure to the South Pole, Shackleton had fallen short.

Chapter 4
South to the Pole—Again

Shackleton was disappointed, but by returning home, he was able to see Emily again. During his trip, her father had died. Although Emily was left plenty of money, Ernest believed that it was his job to support her. He worked first at a magazine, writing about his adventures. Then he got a better job with the Royal Scottish Geographic Society.

Emily and Ernest married on April 9, 1904, in London and moved to Edinburgh, Scotland. With Emily,

Shackleton was as happy as he had ever been. He sent her roses for her birthday in May with this note: "The lovingliest birthday wishes to my darling from her husband."

It seemed as if Shackleton was settling down. Emily was pregnant with Raymond, their first child, who would be born in early 1905.

And then Robert Scott came back from the Antarctic.

After Shackleton had returned in 1903, Captain Scott had spent another year on the icy continent, though he had not reached the South Pole. Scott's return made him a hero. He got a gold medal from the king. The triumphant return of Shackleton's rival put thoughts

ROBERT SCOTT

of another try at the South Pole into Shackleton's head.

He kept working but began to make plans for another expedition. In late 1906, his daughter, Cecily, was born. Now he had two children and a wife to support.

SCOTT OF THE ANTARCTIC

ROBERT FALCON SCOTT WAS A YOUNG BRITISH NAVY OFFICER. IN 1901, HE WAS GIVEN COMMAND OF THE FIRST BRITISH TRIP TO ANTARCTICA. HE WAS A VERY ORGANIZED LEADER, BUT HAD NO EXPERIENCE ON THE ICE.

SOON AFTER SCOTT RETURNED FROM HIS TRIP ON *DISCOVERY* IN 1904, HE BEGAN PLANNING ANOTHER EXPEDITION. REACHING THE ANTARCTIC IN 1911 IN THE *TERRA NOVA*, SCOTT AND THREE OTHERS ONCE AGAIN BEGAN WALKING TO THE SOUTH POLE. THEY ARRIVED THERE IN JANUARY 1912, ONLY THREE WEEKS *AFTER* ROALD AMUNDSEN.

SADLY, SCOTT DIDN'T MAKE IT *BACK* FROM THE SOUTH POLE. HE AND HIS TEAM DIED OF STARVATION AND COLD WHILE TRYING TO RETURN TO *TERRA NOVA*. BEFORE HE DIED, HE LEFT BEHIND LETTERS THAT TOLD HIS TRAGIC STORY.

"FOR MY OWN SAKE, I DO NOT REGRET THIS JOURNEY. . . . WE TOOK RISKS, WE KNEW WE TOOK THEM; THINGS HAVE COME OUT AGAINST US. . . . HAD WE LIVED, [OUR TALE] WOULD HAVE STIRRED THE HEART OF EVERY ENGLISHMAN. [NOW] THESE ROUGH NOTES AND OUR DEAD BODIES MUST TELL THE TALE."

After months of fund-raising, Shackleton had enough money for a second trip to Antarctica.

In early 1907, Shackleton bought a new ship, the *Nimrod*. He hired a crew and bought dogs and ponies for the trip across the ice. He gathered supplies, food, and clothing. He also convinced Emily that the trip would be worth it for the family. He'd earn a fortune writing a book and giving talks when he returned. "Then, sweetheart, we will settle down to a quiet life," he promised.

He would be gone for almost three years.

Before the *Nimrod* set sail, the ship and the crew had visitors. On August 4, 1907, King Edward VII and Queen Alexandra came aboard. Emily and the children were there, too, with Ernest.

"I was very proud" of Ernest, wrote Emily in her diary.

The queen gave the family a British flag and the king gave Shackleton a special award. Not long after, *Nimrod* left England for the Antarctic.

THE DAYS BEFORE FLEECE

TODAY'S POLAR EXPLORERS USE LIGHTWEIGHT AND THIN BUT SUPERSTRONG FABRICS. THEIR CLOTHES KEEP THEM WARM IN EXTREME CONDITIONS. IN SHACKLETON'S DAY, ALL THEY HAD WAS WOOL, FUR, AND SOME OILSKINS AND WINDBREAKERS NOT MUCH THICKER THAN RAINCOATS.

FOR THE *NIMROD* TRIP, SHACKLETON ALSO BROUGHT CLOTHES FROM NORWAY. SLEEPING BAGS WERE MADE FROM REINDEER SKIN, AND MITTENS WERE LINED WITH WOLF AND BEAVER FUR. SPECIAL

REINDEER BOOTS WERE USED, LINED WITH GRASS TO SOAK UP SWEAT. CANVAS AND FUR COATS COVERED THE MEN'S BODIES. THEY ALSO WORE GLASS GOGGLES IN THE ICY WIND. THEY CAMPED IN TENTS OR IN SMALL HUTS MADE OF CORK AND FELT.

TODAY'S EXPLORERS ENJOY SPACE-AGE MATERIALS. THE CLOTHING IS LIGHTER AND WARMER. IT'S SOMETIMES HARD TO IMAGINE HOW THE EARLY EXPLORERS SURVIVED.

Shackleton wrote to Emily sometime later, "I promise that I will take every care and run no risks. I promise you darling that I will come back to you safe."

The *Nimrod* arrived off the shore of Antarctica in early January 1908. The men unloaded 2,500 cases of food and supplies, including a small wood hut. For the next nine months, fifteen men lived in the hut, which was thirty-three feet long and nineteen feet wide—about the size of a school classroom.

At meals, they ate poultry and reindeer, along with fish and stew. They drank lime juice for its vitamin C. To pass the time, the men also listened to a record player and read books.

On Shackleton's thirty-fourth birthday, he was given a letter. Emily had left it with another crew member as a surprise. "I am thinking of you all day long," she wrote. "The children will kiss your photograph night and morning and Ray will pray 'God bless my daddy and bring him safe home to us.'"

He would need those prayers as he set off on the very long walk toward the South Pole. Along with three other men, Shackleton left camp on October 29. The South Pole was the goal—several hundred miles away.

The men and their four ponies trudged through the ice and wind. After twenty-nine days, they had gone farther south than anyone in history. The ponies, however, had not been a good choice. Two died from the cold in the first month alone.

The cold was bitter and painful. The men trudged on for another month, going only a few miles each day. They were getting sick and hungry. Finally, Shackleton had to make a decision, just as Scott had done.

"I must look at the matter sensibly and consider the lives of those who are with me. Man can only do his best," Shackleton wrote in his diary.

Finally, he decided. They would go back to camp without reaching their goal. On January 9, 1909, they put up a British flag in the ice. They were ninety-seven miles from the South Pole. No one had ever come closer. Still, the men were very disappointed.

Surviving on food left behind for the trip back,

they took nearly two months to return to camp. At one point, Shackleton wrote, "Food lies ahead, and death stalks us from behind."

On March 4, they reached camp having traveled nearly 1,700 miles. That was like walking straight through the United States from Canada to Mexico, but with the temperature never above zero!

When Shackleton and the crew of the *Nimrod*

reached London on June 14, 1909, people cheered for them as they rode in cars up the broad avenues. The explorers were heroes! They had *nearly* conquered the South Pole and come back alive. King Edward made Shackleton a Knight of the British Empire.

Sir Ernest happily greeted his family. But "nearly conquering" the South Pole was not good enough for him.

Chapter 5
Outfitting *Endurance*

The *Nimrod* adventure made Shackleton famous. For the next three years, he traveled the world, including the United States, Canada, and Europe. At each stop, he gave speeches about his travels in Antarctica. He also got good news in July 1911; his son Edward had been born.

But while Shackleton was traveling, another explorer realized the very goal he had set for himself. In March 1912, the world heard the news that a team led by Roald Amundsen of Norway had reached the South Pole in December 1911. It had taken Amundsen two months to trek back from the Pole and another month to sail to a place where he could telegraph the news to Europe.

Shackleton was crushed. He had failed in his two attempts and now knew he'd never be the first to reach the South Pole. So Shackleton came up with a different goal for himself. His plan was to walk across the entire continent of Antarctica. His proposed "Imperial Trans-Antarctic Expedition" was a bold idea. Amundsen had barely made it back from the Pole. Scott had lost his life. Shackleton was trying to outdo both of them.

ROALD TO THE POLE

WHEN HE WAS A BOY IN NORWAY, ROALD AMUNDSEN WAS SO SURE HE WOULD BE A POLAR EXPLORER THAT HE SLEPT WITH HIS WINDOWS OPEN ALL WINTER. HE GREW UP TO BE A TALL, POWERFUL LEADER AND ADVENTURER. HE WAS THE FIRST TO GUIDE A SHIP THROUGH THE ICE-ENCRUSTED NORTHWEST PASSAGE NEAR THE NORTH POLE. AFTER SHACKLETON NEARLY REACHED THE SOUTH POLE IN 1909, AMUNDSEN DECIDED HE, TOO, WOULD TRY TO BE THE FIRST MAN TO THE SOUTH POLE.

IN ANTARCTICA, AMUNDSEN USED SPECIAL SLED DOGS. HE CALLED THEM HIS "CHILDREN." FIFTY-TWO DOGS PULLED AMUNDSEN AND HIS TEAM ACROSS THE ICE FOR EIGHT WEEKS. THE POLE CAME

CLOSER AND CLOSER EACH DAY. IT WAS A RACE, INDEED, SINCE ENGLAND'S ROBERT SCOTT WAS ALSO HEADING FOR THE POLE AT THE SAME TIME.

FINALLY, ON DECEMBER 14, 1911, AMUNDSEN'S TEAM REACHED THE SOUTH POLE. THEY WERE THE FIRST MEN TO STAND ON THE BOTTOM OF THE WORLD.

AMUNDSEN RETURNED TO NORWAY TO A HERO'S WELCOME. HE LATER MADE OTHER JOURNEYS IN THE ARCTIC AND ANTARCTIC. TRAGICALLY, HE WAS KILLED IN A PLANE CRASH NEAR THE NORTH POLE IN 1928.

Even with all the dangers, more than five thousand people wanted to go on the trip! It is rumored that three women even wrote to say they would "wear men's clothing" if they got the chance to join the adventure. In the end, Shackleton chose twenty-six men to go with him. They included sailors, scientists, a cook, and doctors.

Shackleton spent months raising money to pay for the trip. The British government donated quite a bit. Friends and family chipped in. Scottish businessman James Caird gave the most. Shackleton used pennies sent by English

schoolchildren to buy sled dogs for the trip. He named some of the dogs for the schools.

Once again, Shackleton left his family behind. He had promised Emily that his *Nimrod* journey would be his last trip, but his love of adventure proved too strong. She could have argued, but she decided to support her husband. He knew how much it hurt her, however. "If you were married to a [stay-at-home] man, you would have been happier, and I also suppose I am just obsessed with my work," he wrote.

In early 1914, he found the ship from Norway that would carry his team south. Shackleton renamed it *Endurance*, meaning the ability to withstand hardship and adversity. It was part of his family's motto: "By endurance we conquer."

On August 3, *Endurance* was ready to set sail. The next day, World War I began in Europe, and England went to war with Germany.

Shackleton called his men together and they took a vote. The South Pole trip could wait if England needed them. Shackleton wrote to the king to volunteer his men and his ship to help in the war. They received a telegram that said, "Proceed." England would fight on without them.

TELEGRAM

...Proceed

Chapter 6
Trapped in the Ice!

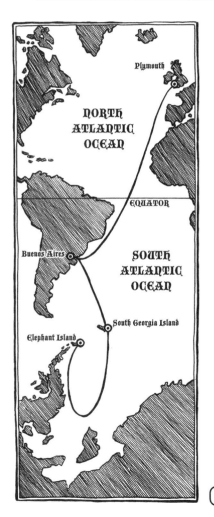

The journey from England to the Antarctic took several months. *Endurance* sailed southwest across the Equator toward South America. It then turned toward the southern tip of the continent. From there, the ship would make the last leg of its journey to Antarctica.

The ship stopped in several places along the way to take on supplies and send mail, which traveled on ships heading back to England. One of *Endurance*'s final stops was at Buenos Aires, Argentina. When the vessel left there, its crew was bigger by one—but Shackleton didn't know it.

Perce Blackboro had snuck aboard the ship as a stowaway. He was not found for several days. The Boss was very upset, but there was nothing he

could do, so Blackboro was given a job helping the ship's cook.

Shackleton jokingly told Blackboro that as the youngest and newest crew member, he would be the first to be eaten if things got really bad.

The rest of the crew were experienced men. Frank Wild was second in command. He had sailed with Shackleton on the *Nimrod*. Tom Crean was second mate. He was a talented sailor who also worked with the sled dogs. Frank Worsley was the captain of the *Endurance*. It was his job to sail the ship south and through the ice.

Other men had special jobs. Scientists studied animal life, the weather, and the rocks and the land. Doctors looked after the men's health. A cook kept them fed. An engineer helped with machines and with building things.

Shackleton kept every man busy with a job, but he also kept them working together. On some ships, officers and men never spoke to each other.

On *Endurance*, every man was made to feel that he was important. At one point later in the trip, for example, Shackleton made sure his crewmen got the best sleeping bags, while his officers took the second-best. His leadership was a big reason the entire crew survived.

After the long trip south, *Endurance* finally arrived at Antarctica in December 1914. They knew they would find ice in the water. Ice surrounds the landmass of the continent of Antarctica. Sometimes that ice field is many miles wide. Even on the land itself, the ice is very thick.

As it turned out, there was much more ice in the water than they expected. For a month, the ship slowly bashed through the icy sea. At times, the men had to climb onto the ice with saws and picks. They chipped away chunks to let the ship move ahead. They carved paths that were like roadways through the ice.

The ship was moving so slowly that penguins could waddle up on the ice to observe it. The men saw whales in the distance as the ship moved slowly on.

But soon, the ship could not move any farther.

ANIMALS OF THE ANTARCTIC

THE ANTARCTIC IS SO COLD THAT NO LAND ANIMALS ACTUALLY LIVE THERE! HOWEVER, THE SURROUNDING OCEANS ARE TEEMING WITH LIFE! AMONG THE FEW BIRDS THAT INHABIT THIS FROZEN LANDSCAPE ARE PENGUINS, INCLUDING THE ROCKHOPPER, KNOWN FOR ITS

ROCKHOPPER PENGUINS

DRAMATIC YELLOW EYEBROWS, AND THE EMPEROR, WHICH CAN GROW TO BE FOUR FEET TALL AND WEIGH AS MUCH AS ONE HUNDRED POUNDS.

ORCAS, ALSO KNOWN AS KILLER WHALES, LIVE AMONG THE ICE PACK AND PATROL THE OCEAN AROUND ANTARCTICA.

A FEW BRAVE BIRD SPECIES, SUCH AS THE ALBATROSS AND THE ANTARCTIC SKUA, MAKE THEIR HOMES IN THE ROCKY CLIFFS AND ISLANDS ON THE EDGES OF THE CONTINENT. WEDDELL SEALS—THE SOUTHERNMOST-DWELLING SEALS IN THE WORLD—REST ON THE ICE DURING FEEDING.

ANTARCTIC SKUA

The ice had crowded in, trapping *Endurance*. They were stuck. The ice pack kept moving in the sea, carrying the ship and the crew farther away from land.

The ship's storekeeper wrote, "We were like an almond in a piece of toffee."

Shackleton rallied his men to refit the trapped

ship as a shelter. He knew they would be there for months. They cleared space and made bedrooms. They named a large room "The Ritz," after a fancy London hotel. The dogs were taken off the ship, zipping down long slides made from sails. "The dogs seemed heartily glad to leave the ship," Shackleton wrote. To shelter the animals, the crew built "dogloos" made of ice.

The men lived on the ship for ten months until late in 1915. They put on plays and read books, and once a month, photographer Frank

Hurley had a slide show. Time passed slowly, and the icy danger was always there.

Shackleton kept his men busy and stayed positive. If Shackleton had not been such a good leader, the time on the ship might have been awful. "He had a genius for keeping his men in good spirits," wrote Blackboro. "He was cheerful at all times. We loved him like a father."

Even The Boss could not stop the ice, however. The huge blocks were slowly crushing *Endurance*. Giant pieces of sharp ice crashed into the sides and cut into the bottom of the ship. The masts were falling and splintering as the ship tilted. The noise from the cracking, crushing ice sometimes kept the men awake. The *Endurance* was made of the strongest wood available. It was more than

140 feet long and weighed 300 tons. But even
it was no match for the power of the ice.

Finally, Shackleton ordered all the men off the

ship for good. They removed all that they could carry as well as the three lifeboats.

On November 21, 1915, Shackleton watched helplessly as *Endurance* sank. The ship had been their home for nearly a year.

Chapter 7
Life at Patience Camp

"Now we'll go home," Shackleton said to reassure his men. He sounded confident, but he knew it would take a long time to make his promise of a return to England come true.

First the crew had to survive on the ice pack until spring. The warmer weather would help melt the ice to reveal the water beneath. Then they could use the small lifeboats to reach nearby islands. Until the ice thawed out, however, Shackleton and his men set up Patience Camp.

The camp was placed on the most solid ice they could find. The men built huts for themselves and new shelters for the dogs. They set aside penguin and seal meat to feed the animals and themselves.

Though they worked hard, they had fun, too. They had dogsled races and they played soccer.

Sports could be dangerous, however. When one sailor chased the soccer ball on the ice, he suddenly fell through! He had to be rescued from the freezing-cold water.

They also faced terrible blizzards. One storm had winds of more than seventy miles per hour with a temperature of thirty-four degrees below zero. Everything froze, including the men's beards.

SOUTHERN LIGHTS

THE MEN IN SHACKLETON'S PARTY SAW ALMOST NOTHING BUT WHITE ICE AND SNOW FOR MONTHS. HOWEVER, ON SOME NIGHTS, THEY WERE ENTERTAINED BY NATURE'S MOST AMAZING LIGHT SHOW. THE SOUTHERN LIGHTS, OR AURORA AUSTRALIS, DANCE IN WAVES ACROSS THE ANTARCTIC SKY. HUGE BANDS OF GREEN, BLUE, OR PURPLE LIGHT SHIMMER AND SHINE IN THE DUSKY AIR. SIMILAR LIGHTS APPEAR AT TIMES NEAR THE NORTH POLE AS WELL, WHERE THEY ARE CALLED THE NORTHERN LIGHTS.

THEY ARE NOT REALLY LIGHTS, BUT A NATURAL PHENOMENON CAUSED BY SUNLIGHT HITTING GAS PARTICLES IN THE ATMOSPHERE. THE DIFFERENT COLORS COME FROM DIFFERENT TYPES OF GAS.

IN ANCIENT TIMES, PEOPLE THOUGHT THE MYSTERIOUS LIGHTS WERE SIGNS FROM THE GODS OR LIGHT FROM FARAWAY CAMPFIRES. VISITORS TODAY TRAVEL THOUSANDS OF MILES FOR A CHANCE TO SEE THE "LIGHTS."

At night, watchmen guarded the camp. They listened for cracking ice. During the day, everyone ate and worked. They didn't wash very often, though. The crew had very little soap, and they had to use snow to clean up! Some men just let the smoke from cooking fires build up on their faces. They thought the layers of soot would help keep them warm.

They hunted seals and penguins to eat, but sometimes it was the other way around. A crewman was walking when a sea leopard leaped out of a hole in the ice and chased him! It nearly

sank its razor-sharp teeth into him. But, luckily, another crew member shot the seal. At more than one thousand pounds, the seal became dinner for several weeks.

Slowly, however, their food supplies shrank. Fortunately, as the weather warmed up, the ice began to shift even more. Soon it might be possible to launch the boats. The men knew that their beloved dogs would not survive the icy voyage. They could not carry enough food to feed dogs and men. They had to make the tough decision to shoot the dogs to add to their food supply.

More than six months after the *Endurance* sank, the ice under Patience Camp began breaking up. The men could feel the ocean rolling under their icy home. Large cracks opened nearby. One swallowed a sailor still in his sleeping bag. Shackleton reached into the water to haul the man out.

The Boss watched the ice and the weather carefully. Finally, on April 9, the final pieces of ice cracked. It was time. Shackleton gave the order they had waited for.

"Strike the tents and clear the boats," he yelled.

Chapter 8
In the Lifeboats

As the ice shattered and cracked around them, Shackleton hustled twenty-seven men into the trio of small boats. The boats were filled with supplies, food, and water. The crew knew that several small islands lay about 120 miles to the northwest. Getting there would be the toughest test so far.

The longest of the boats was almost twenty-three feet, about half as long as a modern school bus. All three were powered by the men using oars. Only one had a mast that could raise a sail.

The waters next to the Antarctic ice pack are very rough. Huge waves lifted the boats up and down. Day after day, the men struggled to row the boats. Some thought they might never make it. One sailor wrote of his fear of being eaten by a killer whale. Other sailors' feet froze so badly they

could not feel them. Frostbite appeared on many fingers.

After seven icy days, they got close to one of the islands. They battled the surf around a small beach. The winds whipped fiercely into their faces. Just as darkness was falling on April 16, Shackleton steered his boat onto the rocky beach. The other two boats followed behind.

They had done it. For the first time in 497 days, the crew of the *Endurance* was on dry land, not ice. The men staggered off the boats. Some flopped down and stared at the sky. Others tore

off their soaking clothes. Some simply sat and said thanks. They had reached Elephant Island, a tiny speck of land in an enormous sea.

Elephant Island was land, but it was not inhabited. Shackleton knew that this barren spot would not support his men for long. They could not wait for help. They had to go find it.

The largest lifeboat, the *James Caird*, was the best for this job. Named for the Scotsman who had helped fund the trip, it had a sail and was the strongest boat. Shackleton picked five men to go with him. He chose second mate Crean, Harry McNeish the carpenter, and sailors Timothy McCarthy and John Vincent. Captain Worsley came to navigate.

The goal was South

CAPTAIN WORSLEY

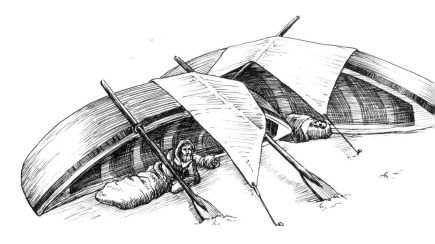

Georgia Island, more than eight hundred storm-tossed miles away.

The rest of the crew would stay on Elephant Island, using the other two boats for shelter. Shackleton gave Frank Wild letters to Emily and his children in case he didn't return.

On April 24, 1916, the *James Caird* left Elephant Island.

The six men had to sail a small, open boat through the roughest seas on the planet. If they didn't make it, not only would they die, but the men on Elephant Island would die, too.

1. *Endurance* Sinks
2. Trip to Elephant Island
3. South Georgia Island
4. Walk across South Georgia Island
5. Return to Elephant Island for other men

Chapter 9
The Greatest Boat Trip Ever

The men raised the sail and headed into the ocean again. The crew left behind on Elephant

Island waved good-bye, not knowing if they would ever see their friends—or The Boss—again.

If the ride to Elephant Island was a challenge, the trip to South Georgia Island was even more difficult. Once again, the sea was very active, with waves towering twenty feet high or more. The wind was fierce. The men worked day and night just keeping the boat moving. "Real rest we had none," Shackleton wrote.

The freezing wind sprayed salt water over everything and the spray iced over. The men had to keep chipping the ice away, because it was making the boat heavier.

The sun hardly ever appeared from behind thick black and gray clouds. That made it even harder for Worsley to navigate properly. If he sent them in the wrong direction, they would be lost forever.

For nine days, they battled the sea, wind, and

ice. On the tenth day, they were hit by the biggest
wave Shackleton had ever seen. It roared over
the tiny boat, filling it with icy water. The men
scooped and bailed. After ten scary minutes, the
James Caird was moving again.

It took them six more days to reach their goal.
The *James Caird* finally slid up the rocky shore of

South Georgia Island. The men had survived one of the most dangerous boat trips ever!

The good news was that a freshwater stream soothed their thirst.

The bad news was that they were on the *wrong* side of the island. The whaling station they were heading for, a camp where whaleboat crews stayed between voyages, was on the far side of the island, seventeen miles away. A mountain of ice, rocks, and snow loomed between the crew and safety.

Chapter 10
The Final Mountain to Climb

The three crewmen from the *James Caird* were too sick to reach the other side of South Georgia Island. Shackleton, Worsley, and Crean were in better shape. They packed light, since they would have to move fast over the steep cliffs and slippery glaciers. McNeish put screws into the soles of the hikers' boots. Pointing outward, the screws would help their feet grip the ice.

Leaving food behind for the three others, Shackleton and his two crewmen began their trek. They climbed over rocks and walked across huge fields of snow. They scaled cliffs and clambered into valleys.

They used ropes to help them climb down steep ice slopes. As they neared the end of their march, they reached the top of a waterfall. They used a rope to lower themselves down—inside the rushing water! It was icy cold, but they knew they *had* to keep moving. They had no shelter available. If they stopped and fell asleep, they would freeze to death.

Finally, after more than thirty-six hours of constant hiking, Shackleton held up a hand. The trio stopped

moving and listened.
Shackleton heard
what he later called
"the sweetest music
human ear had ever
heard." A loud steam
whistle blasted from
the whalers' camp over
the next hill. They had
made it.

On the morning of May 20, 1916, the tired
hikers arrived at the camp. They were covered
in wet, tattered furs, and their faces were ringed
with ice.

The whalers stared at them in amazement.
"Who the devil are you?" they asked.

One of the hikers stepped up and held out his
hand.

"My name," he said, "is Shackleton."

The Boss wasted no time in sending boats

to rescue all his crewmen. First, Worsley took a boat to the other side of South Georgia Island to rescue McCarthy, Vincent, and McNeish. When Worsley arrived, the other *James Caird* sailors didn't recognize him because he had bathed and shaved his beard!

Shackleton himself tried to get back to Elephant Island where the rest of the men from the *Endurance* were stranded. He didn't know if they were alive or dead. Unfortunately, thick ice stopped the rescue ship. Over the next three months, Shackleton tried time and again to reach Elephant Island. Each time, the thick ice forced him back.

During this time, he sent word to England by telegraph that he was safe. King George wrote back, "Rejoice to hear of your safe arrival. Trust your comrades on Elephant Island may soon be rescued." Queen Alexandra sent a telegram to Emily to let her and the children know that Shackleton was alive.

TELEGRAM

Rejoice to hear of your safe arrival. Trust your comrades on Elephant Island may soon be rescued.

Finally, on August 30, 1916, Shackleton made it into the waters off Elephant Island. He looked anxiously toward

the shore. Then he saw a flag on a pole and some small figures. He yelled, "Are all well?"

"We are all well, Boss!" they shouted. "We are all well!"

Chapter 11
The Story of a Leader

Shackleton's family waited three long years
to have him back. Yet life at home felt strange to

him. He had to learn how to be with his children again. Emily wrote to a friend that her husband was used to commanding men on ships. Children could not be ordered around like that.

Shackleton loved his family, but it seemed as if he loved adventure more. Most of his time was spent giving lectures about the *Endurance* trip. Shackleton was forty-seven years old, but he still thought like the young explorer of years earlier. In a letter to Emily, he wrote, "I feel a part of my youth slipping away. I feel I am no use to anyone unless I am out facing the storm." Though he had promised not to leave again, in 1921, he decided to go back to the ice.

For this latest journey, Shackleton hoped to sail around all of Antarctica, with many of the men from the *Endurance* as his crew. The purpose of the trip was to gather scientific information, but most people who knew him thought that Shackleton just wanted one more grand adventure.

Shackleton set sail in the fall of 1921 on the *Quest*. He packed it with all the gear he thought he would need, including a small seaplane. He hoped to make the first flights over the South Pole.

Saying good-bye to Emily and his children once more, Shackleton headed south.

He would never again return home.

During the voyage south on the *Quest*, Shackleton became very sick. He had a heart attack near Brazil, but recovered. The doctors were worried about The Boss. After several months at sea, the *Quest* reached South Georgia Island, the site of the whaling station that Shackleton had reached five years earlier.

Sadly, on January 5, 1922, while the *Quest* lay at anchor off South Georgia, Shackleton had another heart attack. The Boss died that night.

When word reached Emily back in England, she asked that her husband be buried there on

South Georgia. She felt he would want to remain in those cold southern lands he had loved so much.

During Shackleton's lifetime and in the years after his death, the South Pole trips of Amundsen and Scott became more famous than his own. However, in the 1990s, several new books told Shackleton's story for another reason: his leadership. Keeping his crew alive and safe in such terrible conditions showed him to be a great leader. Schools began to study him. People in business thought Shackleton's ideas about teamwork would work for corporations, too.

Shackleton's granddaughter Alexandra played a big part in keeping the story of The Boss alive. In 1999, she helped with a major exhibit at the American Museum of Natural History about Shackleton's seafaring journeys. In 2013, she

funded a group that attempted to re-create the South Georgia boat trip.

But although many dreamed of following in his footsteps, there can only ever be one Sir Ernest Shackleton. He was a brave leader with a driving spirit to conquer the icy unknown.

WHO OWNS ANTARCTICA TODAY?

THE SIMPLE ANSWER IS THAT NO ONE "OWNS" IT. AFTER THE EARLY POLAR EXPLORERS CLAIMED PARTS OF IT FOR THEIR COUNTRIES, LITTLE WAS DONE ABOUT THOSE CLAIMS. IN 1959, A DOZEN COUNTRIES SIGNED THE ANTARCTIC TREATY. THEY AGREED TO SHARE THE ENTIRE CONTINENT AND NEVER TO PUT IT TO ANY MILITARY USE.

SOME NATIONS STILL CLAIM SMALL PARTS OF THE ANTARCTIC, INCLUDING THE UNITED STATES, NORWAY, CHILE, AUSTRALIA, AND ARGENTINA. HOWEVER, THEY LET ALL TREATY NATIONS VISIT AND EXPLORE THEIR LANDS FOR SCIENTIFIC STUDY.

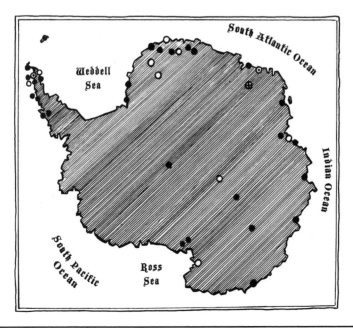

TIMELINE OF
ERNEST SHACKLETON'S LIFE

1874	Ernest Shackleton born in Ireland on February 15
1890	Leaves home to join merchant marine
1898	Earns master's license for all ships
1901-1903	Travels to Antarctica with Robert Scott
1904	Marries Emily Dorman
1905	Son Raymond born
1906	Daughter Cecily born
1907-1909	Shackleton leads *Nimrod* expedition to Antarctic
1911	Son Edward born
1914	Leaves for third Antarctic trip on *Endurance*
1915-1916	Leads ship's crew in survival on pack ice
1916	Makes historic trip to South Georgia to get help
1918	Serves in British army during World War I
1921	Organizes fourth trip to Antarctic
1922	Dies on January 5 and is later buried on South Georgia Island

TIMELINE OF THE WORLD

The American Civil War ends	1865
Thomas Edison invents the phonograph	1878
The volcano at Krakatoa in Indonesia erupts, spreading ash over half the world	1883
The Statue of Liberty is dedicated in New York Harbor	1886
Russian Carsten Borchgrevink takes a ship to Antarctica and becomes the first person to spend a winter there	1898
The Wright brothers make their first flight in North Carolina	1903
Both Robert Peary and Frederick Cook claim to be the first person to reach the North Pole. Their claims are still in dispute today	1909
Roald Amundsen of Norway is the first person to reach the South Pole, just ahead of Robert Scott of England	1911
World War I rages in Europe	1914–1918
Richard Byrd makes the first airplane flight over the South Pole	1929
Twelve nations sign the Antarctic Treaty, pledging to share the continent	1959

BIBLIOGRAPHY

Lansing, Alfred. **Endurance: Shackleton's Incredible Voyage**. New York: Perseus, 2007.

Shackleton, Sir Ernest. **South: The Story of Shackleton's 1914–1917 Expedition**. New York: Carroll and Graf, 1998. (originally published by Shackleton in 1919)

Shackleton, Jonathan and John MacKenna. **Shackleton: An Irishman in Antarctica.** Dublin: Lilliput Press, 2002.

www.amnh.org/exhibitions/past-exhibitions/shackleton
In 1999, the American Museum of Natural History put on a major exhibit about Shackleton and the *Endurance*. The website includes a step-by-step story of the crew's adventures.

www.pbs.org/wgbh/nova/shackleton/
A documentary film about Shackleton gets an online treatment at this site.

www.shackleton-endurance.com
Follow the links from this page to view actual film footage of Shackleton and his crew on the ice and during their entire trip.

www.south-pole.com
This website chronicles and celebrates all the major polar explorers.

www.spri.cam.ac.uk
The Scott Polar Research Archives hold many documents and artifacts from trips by Shackleton and other explorers.